What Was the San Francisco Earthquake?

by Dorothy and Thomas Hoobler

illustrated by Ted Hammond

Penguin Worksho

D0029502

Our sincere thanks to the New York Society Library
for allowing us to use their collection—DH and TH

For my mom—TH

PENGUIN WORKSHOP
An Imprint of Penguin Random House LLC, New York

If you purchased this book without a cover, you should be aware that this book is stolen property. It was reported as "unsold and destroyed" to the publisher, and neither the author nor the publisher has received any payment for this "stripped book."

Penguin supports copyright. Copyright fuels creativity, encourages diverse voices, promotes free speech, and creates a vibrant culture. Thank you for buying an authorized edition of this book and for complying with copyright laws by not reproducing, scanning, or distributing any part of it in any form without permission. You are supporting writers and allowing Penguin to continue to publish books for every reader.

The publisher does not have any control over and does not assume any responsibility for author or third-party websites or their content.

Text copyright © 2016 by Dorothy and Thomas Hoobler. Illustrations copyright © 2016 by Penguin Random House LLC. All rights reserved. Published by Penguin Workshop, an imprint of Penguin Random House LLC, New York. PENGUIN and PENGUIN WORKSHOP are trademarks of Penguin Books Ltd. WHO HQ & Design is a registered trademark of Penguin Random House LLC. Printed in the USA.

Visit us online at www.penguinrandomhouse.com.

Library of Congress Control Number: 2016033767

ISBN 9780399541599 (paperback)   10 9 8 7
ISBN 9780399542121 (library binding)   10 9 8 7 6 5 4 3 2 1

Contents

What Was the San Francisco Earthquake?

On April 18, 1906, at 5:12 a.m., an earthquake ripped through the city of San Francisco. It lasted only forty-seven seconds. But it tore apart hundreds of buildings and streets. Many people were killed in their beds when their houses collapsed. More were injured and would die later. Estimates of the number of people killed range from eight hundred to three thousand.

It was the worst natural disaster in United States history, up to that time. The earthquake caused fires that burned for three days and nights. That led to even more damage and loss of life. About three-quarters of the city's buildings were lost.

In 1906, San Francisco was the greatest American city west of the Mississippi River. It had a population of around four hundred thousand. Surrounded on three sides by water, it was the country's most important Pacific Ocean port. Ships brought fine silks and tea from Asia. California's farm products moved from the port to other countries.

San Francisco had the world's first cable-car system. It carried people up and down the steep hills. But there were no bridges yet connecting San Francisco to nearby cities. Ferries took people across San Francisco Bay to Oakland and Alameda.

The city had many famous neighborhoods, from wealthy Nob Hill to the rowdy center of nightlife called the Barbary Coast. Chinatown was one of the city's oldest neighborhoods. It had the largest Asian-born population in the nation.

Earthquakes had rocked San Francisco before the big one hit. They kept happening because of San Francisco's location. It sits over the San Andreas Fault. The fault is a giant underground crack about 810 miles long. It runs from Humboldt County, California, past the Salton Sea near San Diego. The fault marks the place where two huge tectonic plates meet—the Pacific Plate and the North American Plate.

The earth's crust is made up of many tectonic plates that all move slowly. The Pacific Plate lies under the Pacific Ocean. It heads northwest. The North American Plate moves in the opposite direction.

An earthquake occurs when two plates collide. Pressure builds up over time. Then, the plates suddenly slip and move very fast. There's no way to tell exactly when this will happen.

No one in San Francisco was expecting so great a disaster.

Richter Scale

There was no scale to measure the strength of earthquakes in 1906. In 1935, Charles F. Richter came up with a number scale to describe their force. The scale generally runs from zero to ten. Zero is for no earthquake. After zero, each whole number on the scale represents an earthquake ten times stronger than the number before it. So an earthquake measuring 2.0 is ten times as terrible as one measuring 1.0. Any earthquake above 9.0 destroys nearly all buildings. Based on the damage caused by the 1906 San Francisco earthquake, Richter thought it was an 8.3. (Current technology would probably measure it as a 7.8.)

Charles Richter

CHAPTER 1
The Eve of Destruction

April 17, 1906

The night before the earthquake struck was an important one for San Francisco. The world-famous singer Enrico Caruso was performing at the Tivoli Opera House. Caruso only appeared in big cities, ones that could pay his fee.

Ticket holders arrived at the theater in fancy dress. Men wore tuxedos. The women had on elegant gowns and jeweled "dog collar" necklaces—the latest fashion.

Caruso's voice delighted the audience. The applause went on so long that he took nine curtain calls. No one could have guessed that the beautiful opera house would soon be a burned-out shell.

The Great Caruso

Enrico Caruso was born in Naples in 1873. He first learned to sing in a church choir. His family was poor, so Enrico earned money singing in the street. In his teens, he was hired to sing at cafés and parties. He bought his first pair of new shoes at age eighteen.

Ambitious, he took voice lessons and first appeared onstage at age twenty-two. Five years later, he had a role at Italy's most famous opera house, La Scala. He agreed to make records for the phonograph, a new invention. When people heard them, offers came in from all over the world. In 1903, he sang at the Metropolitan Opera in New York City. He charged up to $10,000 for an appearance. This was a fabulous amount of money at the time.

Record sales made Caruso a millionaire. He loved fine clothes, and traveled with many trunkfuls of them. During World War I, he sang at charity events for free. Worn out from his active life, he died in 1921. But his wonderful voice lives on, even today, in the records he made.

San Francisco had many restaurants that stayed open very late. Caruso went to one that served his favorite pasta. He did not return to his room at the Palace Hotel until after 3:00 a.m.

The Palace Hotel

Others also were up late that night, but not for fun. For firefighters, it was their job to be on duty.

A fire broke out in a warehouse around 11:00 p.m. The fire department responded within minutes. A special alarm system had recently been set up. The bells rang out a code that told exactly where the fire was located.

Each fire station had extra-strong horses that could pull fire trucks up the city's steep hills. That night, firefighter Jack Murray noticed that the horses were unusually nervous. They kicked the sides of their stalls and resisted being put into harness. The horses had been to many fires and never behaved like this. Some people believed animals acted this way before an earthquake. Murray mentioned it to the fire chief, Dennis T. Sullivan.

Dennis T. Sullivan

Sullivan had studied fires in other cities. He knew that San Francisco could be destroyed by a major one. Nine out of every ten buildings were made of wood. Parts of the city were built on new land, made from earth dumped into the San Francisco Bay. So the buildings did not rest on very solid ground. Fires after an earthquake would destroy these areas.

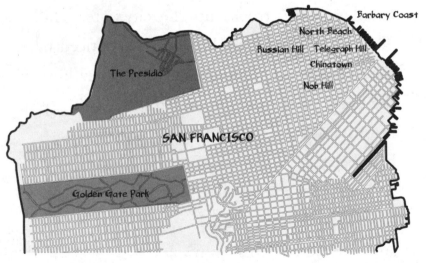

Another problem was the number of tall buildings that now dotted the city's skyline. Some were over three hundred feet high. The water

pressure from the city's hydrants was not strong enough to reach fires on upper floors.

The fire department had pumper trucks that could bring water from the bay. But if a fire was too far from the bay, the pumpers could not be used. There were also *cisterns* (underground tanks of water). However, Sullivan knew that the cisterns were old and leaky. They would not be much help in a major fire.

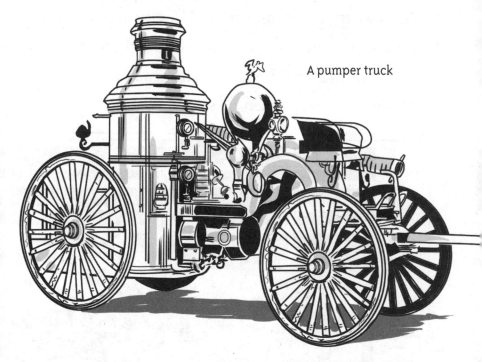

A pumper truck

In other cities, fire departments sometimes used dynamite to fight major fires. Destroying buildings in the path of the fire kept it from spreading. Sullivan had asked to train a team to use dynamite for large fires in San Francisco. But city officials always said there wasn't enough money to pay for that.

So when Sullivan heard about the nervous horses, the chief just shook his head. Something else to worry about tomorrow. After the warehouse fire was put out, he went home to the fire station, where he and his wife lived. The chief was never off duty, not even when he slept.

Animals and Earthquakes

The ancient Greeks were the first to notice that animals sometimes acted strangely before earthquakes. Chickens stopped laying eggs. Bees deserted their hives. But so far, there is no scientific proof to back up these stories.

What reason could there be for animals sensing an oncoming quake? Scientists have found that smaller waves, called *P-waves*, occur before the main force of an earthquake hits. It is possible that animals can sense these P-waves, while humans cannot.

Research is being done in China and Japan, two countries that have had many earthquakes. In 1975, Chinese officials ordered the people of Haicheng to leave the city. More than a million people lived there. The order was based on reports that animals were acting strangely. A few days later, an earthquake did occur. It measured 7.3 on the Richter scale. Many thousands of people were saved because they had already left the area.

CHAPTER 2
The Earth Dragon Awakes

April 18, dawn

The fire department horses had indeed sensed something.

At dawn, the earthquake began. It traveled at an average speed of more than two miles a second!

(About seven thousand miles an hour.) It began two hundred miles north of the city, breaking apart giant redwood trees as if they were matchsticks. It buckled steel railroad tracks, throwing a train into the air.

On one farm, a cow was swallowed up by the earth as a crack opened and then closed again, leaving only the cow's tail showing. A ship one hundred fifty miles offshore rose out of the water. The captain and crew thought they had hit a whale.

Then the quake reached San Francisco.

John Barrett, a newspaper editor, was on his way home. Suddenly he heard a long, low moaning sound. He began to have trouble walking. "It was as if the earth was slipping gently from under our feet. Then came a sickening swaying of the earth that threw us flat upon our faces."

All around him, Barrett saw buildings rocking back and forth "in what looked like a crazy dance . . . Big buildings were crumbling as one might crush a biscuit in one's hand."

To live through a major earthquake is a terrifying experience. When the ground under you moves, where can you feel safe? If a building might fall down on top of you, where can you go?

When Barrett could stand again, he saw that "Trolley tracks were twisted, their [electric] wires down, wriggling like serpents, flashing blue sparks all the time. The street was gashed in any number of places. From some of the holes water was spurting; from others, gas."

Church bells all over the city began to ring. No one was pulling their ropes. The bell towers were swaying from the earthquake. The walls of the new city hall came crashing to the ground. Oddly, its huge dome remained standing on top of a framework of steel. It was just one of hundreds of buildings that collapsed in the first moments of the disaster.

The ruins of City Hall

Another was the California Hotel. It stood next to the fire station where Chief Sullivan lived. In the first seconds of the quake, the chief rushed to his wife, who was asleep in the next room. It was pitch-dark. The chief could not see that the top of the hotel had broken through the firehouse roof. It had crashed down three more floors to the basement. Mrs. Sullivan's bed, with her in it, fell into the hole. So did the chief.

The other firefighters hurried to rescue them. Mrs. Sullivan was not badly hurt. The mattress on the bed had saved her. But the chief was knocked out cold and was rushed to a hospital. The person who knew the most about earthquakes and fires was out of action.

In Chinatown, the Lowe family lived above their restaurant. Mrs. Lowe was awakened by the rattling of pots and pans. She thought the cook was making breakfast. Then the brick wall next to her bed fell down. She scooped up her children and fled outside. People in the street were shouting, "Day Loong Jun Ah!" which means, "The Earth Dragon awakes." That was what Chinese people called earthquakes.

CHAPTER 3
No Place Is Safe

April 18, morning

As soon as the shaking stopped, most people ran outside. The streets soon filled with crowds in pajamas and nightgowns. Arnold Genthe, a photographer, passed a man wearing just a nightshirt. A friendly policeman told him, "Say, Mister, I guess you better put on some pants."

Many other people never escaped from their homes. They were crushed underneath tons of stone and bricks even before they could get out of bed.

The cries of trapped victims filled the air. Rescuers started to dig into the wreckage with their bare hands. But even when the wounded were freed, it was hard to get help for them. The city's hospitals quickly became overcrowded with victims.

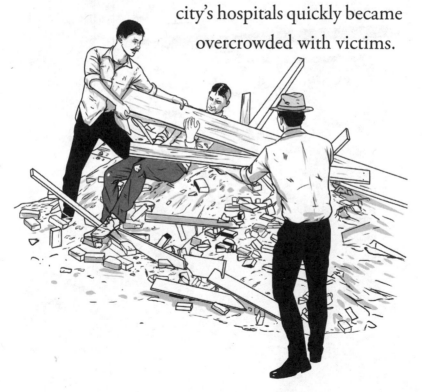

Enrico Caruso was still in bed when the quake first hit. Alfred Hertz, Caruso's music conductor, rushed to Caruso's hotel room. Hertz persuaded him to get dressed and go outside. Caruso left trunks of clothes behind. All he took was an autographed photograph of President Theodore Roosevelt. Caruso said it would be his ticket to safety.

Unlike Caruso, Hazel Yardley didn't know any important people. She was a poor widow and had been shopping at a farmers market. When the earthquake was over, she rushed back to her apartment to find her daughter. The building was now nothing but a heap of bricks. Hazel began to claw through them, searching for her child. Neighbors finally pulled her off, telling her that the daughter was lost. Hazel walked away, clutching the only thing she could find: a photo of the girl. She kept showing it to people, asking if they had seen her.

In the streets of Chinatown, an escaped bull ran loose. People were terrified. Some Chinese people believed in a myth that the world rested on the backs of four great bulls. The runaway bull was a sign that the world was falling apart. A policeman came and shot the bull. That didn't seem like a good omen, either.

A newspaper reporter recalled, "The streets were full of people, half-clad . . . but silent, absolutely silent, as if suddenly they had become speechless idiots . . . I saw many men and women with gray faces. No one spoke. All of them had a singular hurt expression . . . as if some trusted friend had suddenly wronged them."

And the worst was not over. Soon there was a new threat to face—fire.

Arnold Genthe, Photographer

Arnold Genthe came to the United States from Germany in 1895, when he was twenty-six. He learned photography and opened a studio in San Francisco. He found the city's Chinatown a fascinating place. The photographs he took there are among the only pictures left of the neighborhood before the great earthquake.

When Genthe's studio burned down after the quake, all of his pictures were destroyed except for the Chinatown ones. He had put them in storage

because a friend had warned there would be a great fire one day. The friend thought the photos were too important to leave in the studio. Today, most of Genthe's pictures of Chinatown are in the Library of Congress in Washington, DC.

CHAPTER 4
Fire!

April 18, noon

So what caused the terrible fires?

Underground gas lines. They were torn apart, and the leaking gas reached sparks from fallen electric lines. It exploded into flame. Fires began to break out all over the city. Unfortunately, the city's new fire-alarm system was destroyed. So local fire stations had to wait to hear about fires before they could respond to them.

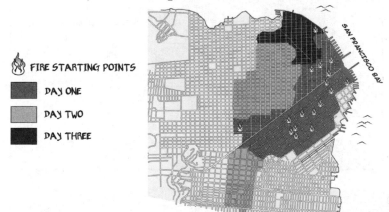

FIRE STARTING POINTS

DAY ONE

DAY TWO

DAY THREE

SAN FRANCISCO BAY

When firefighters did arrive, they found broken water pipes. Hydrants were dry. To fill their hoses, the fighters had to pump water from cisterns deep underground. But many of the cisterns were empty, too.

The first fires were south of Market Street, the wide avenue nicknamed the Slot. Clouds of smoke rose into the air. New blazes were starting all the time. Early that morning, a woman who lived near Market Street started to make breakfast.

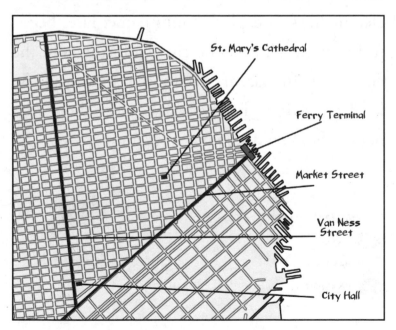

St. Mary's Cathedral

Ferry Terminal

Market Street

Van Ness Street

City Hall

Her broken stovepipe kindled a fire that spread through the neighborhood. It became known as the "ham and eggs" fire. It took firefighters all day just to put out this one blaze. It destroyed thirty blocks. And more fires were breaking out all the time.

By noon, the fires throughout the city were out of control.

A telegraph operator tapped out the message: "THEY ARE CARTING DEAD FROM THE FALLEN BUILDINGS. FIRE ALL OVER TOWN. THERE IS NO WATER AND WE LOST OUR POWER. I'M GOING TO GET OUT OF THE OFFICE AS WE HAVE HAD A LITTLE SHAKE EVERY FEW MINUTES AND IT'S ME FOR THE SIMPLE LIFE." This was how the outside world first learned of the quake.

What the telegraph operator called "little shakes" were *aftershocks*. These are smaller, shorter quakes that follow a major one. The first aftershock lasted more than ten seconds. It would have been at least a 6 on the Richter scale. In other words, a big quake. There were seventeen aftershocks on Wednesday. They continued for at least a week.

The mayor of San Francisco, Eugene Schmitz, had never faced anything like this. On hearing that the saloons were filled with people drinking, the mayor gave his first order: Close all bars. People were also breaking into stores and homes and stealing whatever they found. Mayor Schmitz ordered that looters should be shot on sight.

Army General Frederick Funston also tried to control the situation. He was commander of a fort called the Presidio. As soon as the earthquake was over, Funston ordered his soldiers to march into the city to keep order.

General Funston also decided to fight the fires. He planned to use dynamite. His men would blow up

General Frederick Funston

houses in the path of the flames. That would create an empty area that the fire could not spread across.

It was the same as Fire Chief Sullivan's plan. But Sullivan had wanted a trained team to carry it out. Not General Funston's soldiers. Though Funston had no dynamite, he was so eager to start that his men used gunpowder instead.

This was more powerful than they expected. The first blast sent burning pieces of wreckage into nearby Chinatown. The old wooden buildings there were soon on fire.

All Funston did was make a terrible situation worse.

CHAPTER 5
Escape!

April 18, early afternoon

Soon, thousands of people were fleeing the city. The best way seemed to be on the ferryboats that went across the bay to Oakland or Alameda.

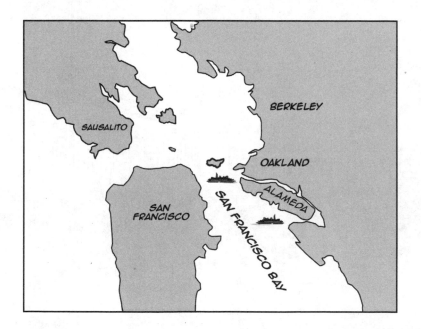

People rushed to the ferry terminal at the end of Market Street. But the crowds were too large for everyone to get on board. One eyewitness wrote, "At the iron gates they clawed with their hands [like] so many maniacs . . . When the ferry drew up . . . and the gates were thrown open the rush to safety was tremendous. The people flowed through the passageway like a mountain torrent . . ."

Soon the fires threatened the ferry terminal. Tugboats with hoses sent streams of water onto the building. As the fires spread closer to Market Street, it became too dangerous to walk along there. Soldiers began turning people back.

Some gathered at the Presidio on the northern tip of the city. Others headed for Golden Gate Park on the western side. Three miles long and half a mile wide, it was the largest city park in the United States. People often went there to relax. Now it promised safety, for it had plenty of open green spaces.

Of course, getting to the park was very hard. Twisted tracks made streetcars useless. The cobblestone streets were a wreck. Huge holes made it hard for horse-drawn wagons to travel. So people dumped their possessions in baby carriages, toy wagons, and homemade carts. They dragged trunks mounted on roller skates.

Those who remained in their homes tried to prepare for fire. They filled containers with water. In the Italian neighborhood in North Beach, people used barrels of homemade wine instead. But General Funston told the soldiers to force people out of their houses. He ordered them to

use guns or bayonets, if necessary.

Everywhere, the city was tense. Surviving the earthquake had not been enough. Now people had to escape the fires—fires that showed no sign of ending.

CHAPTER 6
Deeds of Bravery

April 18, late afternoon

Jack London, San Francisco's most famous writer, feared the worst. "I knew it was all doomed," he wrote. "By Wednesday afternoon . . . half the heart of the city was gone." As he watched, the heat from the fires created strong winds that spread the flames faster.

Even so, firefighters fought on, often helped by

Jack London

soldiers and volunteers. They searched desperately for sources of water. They pumped it from sewers, from pools on construction sites, and from the ocean and bay. When they had no water, they tried to beat out the flames with their heavy coats and blankets. It was a backbreaking job.

In some places, people helped save the buildings where they worked. One was the US Mint, where gold and silver were stored. A well for fighting fires had recently been installed. Unfortunately, the quake had broken its pump.

Finally, the pump was repaired. Mint employees took hoses to the roof and sprayed water over it. On the lower floors, people with buckets of water put out small fires before they could spread. Later that day, the fire passed by, sparing the Mint. All around it, other buildings had burned to the ground.

Near the Mint was the new US [...]
Many people thought it was the mo[...]
building in San Francisco. Though po[...]
were told to go home, many remained. To prevent
any sparks from catching fire, workers tore down
curtains and moved furniture away from windows.
They soaked empty mailbags in water and used
them to block
broken windows.
They, too, won
their fight to save
their workplace.
Not only that,
every piece of
mail at the post

office was eventually delivered. Later on, letters
without stamps were delivered. People had sent
them to tell friends they were safe. The post office
even accepted messages written on scraps of paper
and shirt collars.

Sadly, most of the business district went up in flames. The offices of the city's newspapers fell victim to the fire. One was the *San Francisco Call* building. At eighteen stories high, it was the tallest building in the city. It was one of the skyscrapers Chief Sullivan had worried about. The windows of the building shattered, fanning flames that made the temperature inside rise to 2,000°F. Even the window frames melted. Though the shell of the building remained standing, everything inside was destroyed.

Moshe Cohen was a photographer at the *Call*. He escaped and went to a small park. People had abandoned some possessions there. He found sugar, coffee, and bread, and decided they shouldn't go to waste. He discovered a well in a nearby garden. He built a fire and made coffee. With discarded cups from the park, he opened a makeshift "restaurant." As weary people passed by, he offered them "as much as you like for nothing." That was only one example of the spirit that would save San Francisco.

CHAPTER 7
Blasts in the Night

April 18–19, overnight

By nightfall of the first day, the fire had crossed Market Street and headed north. People could now get to the ferry again. Word also spread that the Southern Pacific Railroad was offering free tickets from Oakland to anyplace in the United States. That was a tempting offer.

General Funston wanted fewer people in the city. So he issued an order. Anyone who left the city could not return. Funston was operating on his own. He seldom consulted with Mayor Schmitz, who was not a strong leader.

All the mayor did was appoint a committee of fifty citizens to help him figure out what to do.

Mostly, the committee sent out proclamations— orders that were supposed to apply to everyone.

The mayor heard that children were stealing from abandoned stores. He ordered that any child caught stealing should be beaten and forced to wear a sign reading I AM A THIEF. This was hardly the worst problem the city faced. There is no evidence that the order was ever carried out.

Some people refused to leave the city. Among them were the residents of Chinatown. Fire had swept through the twelve-block area, forcing everyone to flee. "They carried their bundles,"

reported a Chinese newspaper, "walking away but at the same time looking back as they did so, brooding or weeping softly. They camped in the open as did people of all colors, all ages, all sexes, both rich and poor."

In other neighborhoods, houses remained standing after the quake. Residents thought the fires would not reach them. But the flames never slowed down, and more homeless people were constantly joining the crowds looking for safety.

At Golden Gate Park and the Presidio, thousands of people had gathered by Wednesday night. General Funston was prepared to shelter twenty thousand people in tents. But there were at least 225,000 homeless. Many of them had to sleep on the grass. The soldiers began to pass out food. Long lines formed. Grocery owners gave away whatever they had. Still, many people went to bed hungry.

It was difficult for anyone to sleep that night. Fires lit up the sky so brightly that people could read by the light. The city looked like a furnace. And all night long, there were explosions. General Funston had gotten some dynamite now, and his men were using it freely—too freely, some

thought. But Funston felt that if the fires were not stopped, the entire city could burn.

When dawn came, people saw that the fires had spread farther. Clouds of smoke turned the sky black. Many agreed with Jack London that the city was doomed.

CHAPTER 8
Rich and Poor

April 19, morning and afternoon

Until Thursday, the city's hilltops had been spared from the fires. Nob Hill was where the city's most powerful families lived. Yet twenty-four hours after the earthquake, fire reached the area. The homes of the four richest families in San Francisco were consumed by flames. These houses had been as lavish as castles. They were filled with artwork, rare books, and furniture. But nothing could withstand the power of the fires.

The plain truth was that fire destroyed the lives of the rich as well as the poor. The Barbary Coast was the neighborhood where criminals

and pleasure-seekers gathered at night. It, too, fell
to the fire, which swept through streets nicknamed
Dead Man's Alley and Murder Point.

By Thursday afternoon, much of the eastern half of the city lay in ruins. General Funston advised Mayor Schmitz to make a stand against the fire at Van Ness Avenue. That was the city's main north-south street. Many of the city's finest homes were located there. But Funston said that destroying them to make a fire wall was the only way to save the western part of the city. Finally, the mayor agreed.

Funston's men drove people from houses on the east side of Van Ness. Then the soldiers began to destroy the homes. This time, they used not only dynamite but also cannons. All over the city, people were jolted by the noise. It sounded like a war.

Soldiers even set fires on purpose. James Stetson, who lived west of Van Ness, watched through a telescope. He saw soldiers entering houses with containers of kerosene. They climbed to an upper floor, opened the windows, and set fire to the curtains. The plan was to get rid of everything in the fire's path. Stetson doubted the plan would work.

A soldier forced Stetson out of his own home at the point of a bayonet. The soldier insisted the house was in danger from the fire. Stetson was sure he was wrong. When no one was watching, he sneaked back in. But the fire drew nearer, and

Stetson began to worry. After he saw a small fire on the roof next door, he offered ten dollars to anyone who would help put it out. Someone did. Only one house around Stetson's burned. His house remained safe, too.

E. A. Dakin also succeeded in saving his home. A Civil War veteran, Dakin had a flag collection. When the fire got too close, he raised the largest flag over his house. He dipped it three times—a sign of farewell.

A group of soldiers saw the flag dip. They stopped at Dakin's house and worked to save it. Part of the house, four stories up, began to smolder. Five soldiers climbed to the roof. They held one man by his ankles and lowered him so he could reach the blaze. He used a seltzer bottle to put out the fire.

General Funston's drastic action did stop the fire from crossing Van Ness. At least for now, most of the western area of the city was safe. But the avenue was four miles long, and the fire could not be stopped everywhere. Many fires were still burning in other parts of San Francsico. The job was far from over.

The Big Four of San Francisco

The "Big Four" was a popular nickname for the four men who built the western part of the railroad that ran across the United States. In 1862, Congress had passed a bill giving land and money to two companies to build the railroad. One would start in Omaha, Nebraska, and work west. The other would start in Sacramento, California, and head east.

The Central Pacific Railroad Company was formed by four San Francisco shopkeepers—Leland Stanford, Collis Huntington, Mark Hopkins, and Charles Crocker. They wanted their railroad builders

Leland Stanford, Collis Huntington, Mark Hopkins, and Charles Crocker

to work faster than the other company's because each railroad was paid for every mile of track it laid. So the project became something like a race.

Crocker suggested hiring Chinese immigrants. Many had come to California during the gold rush of 1849. The Chinese laborers worked so hard that the railroad company started bringing more people from China itself. They were paid a dollar a day.

The Big Four became fabulously wealthy. They used some of their money for charities. Together, they established a state library. Leland Stanford and his wife, Jane, started Stanford University in honor of their only child, a son who had died young.

CHAPTER 9
Hope

April 19, afternoon and evening

On Thursday afternoon, the lines along Market Street to the ferry grew even longer. People were desperate to get to Oakland. There was no room for possessions on the ferry. So they had to leave everything behind. Still, one man brought a trained rat. He said it was like his son. The ferry operator let him bring it along.

In one line was Enrico Caruso. He had paid a man three hundred dollars to carry him to the ferry in a wagon. Now, he showed his picture of President Roosevelt to the ferry operator. "I am Enrico Caruso, the friend of your president," Caruso said. "I must leave the city at once."

The operator looked him over. "If you're Caruso, prove it," he said. "Sing."

Earlier, Caruso had feared that the earthquake had damaged his voice. Now he had to sing for his life. So he took a deep breath and began to sing one of the arias from *Carmen*.

People standing nearby applauded. "That's Caruso, all right," one of them said. "Let him on the boat."

So the picture of President Roosevelt proved to be his ticket to safety, after all.

Another ferry passenger was Hazel Yardley. She was still showing around the picture of her missing daughter. A policeman had told her that homeless children were in a refugee camp in Oakland. When Hazel arrived, she came to a tent where a young couple was cooking stew. After they saw the picture, the husband went inside and carried out a sleepy little girl. It was Annie Yardley, safe and sound. The couple had found her after the earthquake and brought her along with their own children. Mrs. Yardley was Catholic and the couple was Jewish. Together they gave thanks that Hazel's prayers had been answered.

Back in San Francisco, the firefighters were weary. Most had worked without sleep for almost two days. Some of them dropped where they stood and had to be carried off. Many firehouses had burned down, and hundreds of the firefighters were now homeless, too.

But they finally had water. They were able to pump a thousand gallons of water a minute out of the bay. The fire department of Oakland came to help out.

The wind changed course. That was a good sign. It blew the flames back over areas that had already been burned. But much of the city remained ablaze. As night fell, the flames still lit up the sky. No one felt safe.

Romance in the Disaster

San Francisco had a large fleet of fishing boats. Many of them started to take people across the bay. On one boat were Giuseppe Alioto and thirteen-year-old Domenica Lazio. The two became friends, and ten years later were married. In 1968, their son, Joseph Alioto, became mayor of San Francisco. Mayor Alioto was responsible for a citywide plan to prepare for the next major earthquake.

CHAPTER 10
To the Edge of Defeat

April 20

Friday morning was the beginning of the third day of the fires. Moshe Cohen, the photographer, had used up all his film. He went to a high point to see what was happening below. "The whole city seemed to be drowning in flame," he remembered. "And not just ordinary flames, but whole waves of orange and red and purple and yellow, all mixed up together with a terrible dense smoke . . . Flame and smoke seemed to have a life of their own . . . with a sound that nobody had heard before. It wasn't normal fire sounds, for sure. No, this was a *chattering*, like a billion monkeys."

What Cohen saw and heard was a *firestorm*. In huge fires like this one, the heat causes air to rise and make the fire even hotter until everything inside it explodes.

At Telegraph Hill, most people had not abandoned their homes. Many were *immigrants*— people who had recently come to America. They lived in small wooden houses, which they defended against the flames. An eyewitness wrote about their victory: "It was the boys of the hill that saved the hill . . . Tim O'Brien, who works in the warehouse at the foot of the hill, and his brother Joe, who works in a lumberyard . . . It was the old Irishwomen who had hoarded a few buckets of water through the long days of fear and rumor . . . It was the poor peasant Italian with a barrel of cheap wine in his cellar who now sweatily rolled it out and . . . fought the fire till he dropped . . . It was Sadie who works in the box factory and Annie who is a coat finisher and Rose who is a chocolate dipper in a candy shop." Together, they beat the fire back and saved Telegraph Hill. In doing so, they helped save the waterfront, which was just beyond the hill.

The fire was still threatening to cross another section of Van Ness Avenue. The mayor now took a firm stand. He demanded that the army stop blowing up buildings, and General Funston obeyed.

So it was up to the exhausted firefighters to carry on the fight alone. They seemed ready to give up. But what would happen if they did?

The mayor had appointed a new fire chief to take Sullivan's place. His name was John Dougherty. Usually a soft-spoken man, he now stormed up and down the avenue, shouting at his men. He said he was ashamed of them. They were all younger than he was, and here they were ready to quit.

A reporter wrote, "The firemen swore they would make Dougherty eat his words. They took a new grip on the hoses and drove their streams hard into the flames . . . They would rather take a bellyful of smoke and flame than admit to the old man that he could stand the punishment longer than they could."

The Miriam and Ira D. Wallach Division of Art, Prints and Photographs: Photography Collection, The New York Public Library.

A busy street before the earthquake

People walking on Market Street toward the Ferry Building

© Bettmann/Getty Images

Smoke from the fires billowing over the city

H. D. Chadwick/National Archives and Records Administration

The intersection of Post Street and Grant Avenue

George Williford Boyce Haley/National Archives and Records Administration

People trying to leave San Francisco

Chadwick, H. D./National Archives and Records Administration

The Mission District burning

Arnold Genthe/Library of Congress

Watching the fires from Sacramento Street

Wikimedia Commons

The Mark Hopkins Mansion on Nob Hill

U.S. Federal Government

Soldiers patrolling the devastation

A refugee camp in Jefferson Square

The Golden Gate Park camp

An improvised kitchen on the street

© Paul Sakuma/Associated Press

The 1989 earthquake buckled a highway.

FEMA News Photo

Men stand where a street has been cut in half.

J.K. Nakata/United States Geological Survey

A crushed car under a collapsed building

© Jonathan Nourok/Getty Images

People on the street in 1989 looking at the damage

San Francisco as seen from the bay today

A view of downtown San Francisco

© 8grapher/Thinkstock

© Encrier/Thinkstock

© Tony Webster/Wikimedia Commons

A street in modern-day Chinatown

The Ferry Building today

© Cosmonaut/Thinkstock

They put out the fire with heroic efforts. The area west of Van Ness was saved for good.

St. Mary's Cathedral, one of the city's largest churches, was on Van Ness. Father Charles Ramm was a young priest working there. Silently, he had promised to give his own life to save the cathedral. And on Friday morning, just before noon, a tongue of flame could be seen at the top of the church steeple. The fire hoses could not reach it.

Father Ramm realized what he had to do. He began to climb the steeple, with a bag around his neck. A crowd gathered below. People began to shout at him to come down. But he wouldn't. Desperately clinging to the side of the steeple, he made his way upward. At last he reached the fire, and beat it out with the bag. A reporter wrote, "For a moment the crowd did nothing. Then somebody shouted that we had just witnessed a miracle."

CHAPTER 11
The Fires Die

April 21–22

As the third day after the earthquake dawned, the battle for San Francisco went on. Some fires continued to spread through the southern section of the city. Early Saturday morning, a man discovered a hydrant there that still had water. A hose was hooked up to it, and the last flames were put out. (For many years after that, the hydrant was painted gold as a memorial.)

Now the only real threat was along North Beach, in the northeast tip of the city. The fire there was particularly dangerous because it might reach oil tanks along the piers. If that happened, there would be a mammoth explosion.

Fortunately, US Navy ships arrived. President Theodore Roosevelt had sent them when he heard of the disaster. Their crews came ashore to help the city fire department. A fireboat sprayed water over the area. At last, at 7:15 a.m., seventy-four hours after the earthquake, the last of the fires flickered and then died. It was over.

In a little while, it started to rain.

The fire was over, but at least half of the city's people had lost their homes. The parks were filled with families who lived in tents. (They put up joking signs, like "The New Palace Hotel.") But their future was uncertain. They did not know if they would have jobs. The central business district was nothing but ashes.

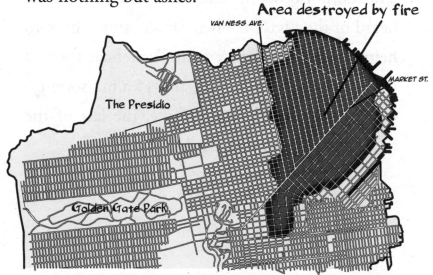

Yet everyone felt the need to give thanks. Much of the city remained. The docks, which were necessary for its economy, had been saved. And people were grateful just to be alive.

On Sunday, the archbishop of San Francisco said mass at St. Mary's Cathedral. The service was held outdoors. The fire department said it was still not safe inside. So hundreds gathered in the street in front of St. Mary's to pray. The archbishop had sad news to deliver. He told the crowd that Fire Chief Sullivan had died. He never regained consciousness. He never knew of the bravery of the firefighters he had trained.

In Golden Gate Park, the Presidio, and other places, people gathered for prayer services. There was a sense that everyone had been through the worst and could now look to the future. There were already signs that the city was recovering. Children were being born in Golden Gate Park. Many of them were named Golden Gate, and had a story to tell all their lives.

Somebody posted a sign on a ruined building: "There is no water and still less soap. We have no city, but lots of hope."

There is no water and still less soap.

We have no city

but lots of hope.

A Friendly Banker

A. P. Giannini was the head of a small bank called the Bank of Italy. Most of his customers were Italian

A. P. Giannini

immigrants. Right after the earthquake, Giannini feared that the money in his bank would be burned or stolen. He borrowed a wagon and took all the money to his home, south of the city.

After the fires were out, Giannini set up a wooden stand near Washington Square. He had a bag of gold coins with him and began making loans. People needed money to rebuild their homes and businesses.

Giannini's Bank of Italy was the first bank to reopen after the quake. The safes in the bigger banks

were too hot to open for days. (Remember, there were no ATMs at that time.) Giannini's customers remembered how he'd been willing to take a chance by loaning money to them. So in the months ahead, they began to deposit any money they had in Giannini's bank. Later on, he changed the name to Bank of America. It still exists today and is one of the world's largest banks.

CHAPTER 12
Rebuilding

The days after

On a billboard at the edge of Golden Gate Park, people started to post messages. They wrote their names and where they were staying. That way, families and friends could find one another.

Food and water were the most necessary things. The Red Cross started to open community kitchens. They provided hot meals for people who still had no homes.

Conditions in the camps were often unhealthy. Thousands of rats had fled the burning buildings. They spread illnesses among the families in the parks.

Army engineers built wooden barracks in the parks so people could move out of the tents. The people who lived in these barracks put up signs giving the family name, along with their old street and house number. Postal workers started to make lists of these, so they would know where to deliver the mail.

By May, stores began to reopen. However, it took years before the city recovered fully. The buildings that went up right after the disaster were still not fully prepared for earthquakes. Not until later did engineers develop better construction methods.

Some areas, like Chinatown, were quicker to rebuild than others. City officials wanted to move the Chinese people farther away from the center of town. Fortunately, before this plan could be carried out, Chinese residents were already at work. They rebuilt the homes and businesses they had lost. Today, San Francisco's Chinatown is right where it was before the quake.

Not everyone was able to recover. A homeless man with a broken leg told Jack London, "Last night I was worth thirty thousand dollars . . . now all I own are these crutches." Many others had similar stories. They'd lost everything. The total damage was estimated at $400 million. That would be more than $8 billion in today's money.

As for how many people died, the number couldn't be counted. Estimates range from the hundreds to the thousands. Bodies had been burned up and disappeared in the fire. Soldiers had buried others where they found them. Also, city records were destroyed, records that showed who lived in San Francisco before the earthquake. Without those records, it was impossible to account for who had died or left the city.

Some people decided to make a fresh start elsewhere. That is why the population of the city dropped for a time. It fell from 400,000 to a low of 110,000 by June.

But many returned. As a sign of the city's rebirth, San Francisco continued with plans to hold a world's fair in 1915. The fair opened on time. One of its tallest buildings was the Tower

of Jewels, which was covered with bits of colored glass. San Francisco nicknamed itself "The Jewel City." It had taken its place once again as a great and exciting place to live and visit.

Searching for a Bride

The morning of the earthquake, Henry Lai had arrived by train from Cleveland, Ohio. He was Chinese, and was coming to marry Yuen Kum. She lived with a group of students. Henry had proposed to her by mail. Yuen had accepted, and their wedding was scheduled for Sunday.

Henry made his way through the broken streets to Chinatown, where Yuen lived. People there had already fled from the fire. For the next three days, Henry wandered around the wrecked city. Every time he saw a Chinese face, he asked about Yuen.

He finally learned from a minister that Yuen's school had gone to San Anselmo, across the bay. Henry lined up with the thousands of people waiting for the ferry. He was the last person through the gate on his trip.

Henry's persistence paid off. He found Yuen. On Sunday, in a chapel in San Anselmo, the young couple was married. Yuen's teacher wrote, "Just after the wedding, Mr. and Mrs. Henry Lai started for their home in Cleveland amidst showers of California roses . . . So romance with its magic touch helped us for a time to forget our great loss."

CHAPTER 13
Can It Happen Again?

San Francisco cannot change the fact that, like much of California, it sits on the San Andreas Fault. The two plates on either side keep on moving one or two inches a year. So that means there is always the possibility of earthquakes. Fortunately, none of the earthquakes since the one in 1906 have been as severe.

The worst struck in October 1989. People all over the nation saw it happen. How? They had their TVs on to watch a World Series game at San Francisco's Candlestick Park. All of a sudden the picture went off, but the announcers stayed on the air. They told viewers that an earthquake had just struck. Within minutes, cameras showed a collapsed bridge and major fires. A TV news reporter appeared in the parking lot of the ballpark. He described the shaking. Viewers held their breath, wondering if the stadium would fall. It did not, but there was major damage all over the area. (You can see a replay on YouTube.)

Hardest hit were the San Francisco Marina District, which had been built on artificial land, and the city of Santa Cruz, where many buildings were between fifty and one hundred years old. Ten bridges were damaged so badly that they had to be closed. In all, the 1989 quake caused sixty-three deaths and did $6 billion in property damage.

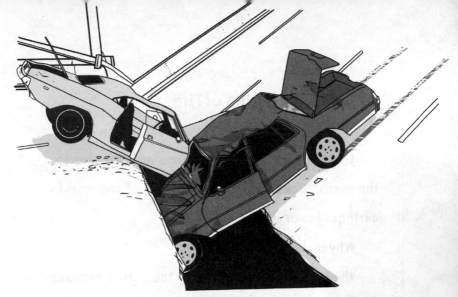

The 1989 quake measured 6.9 on the Richter scale. But the damage was not as bad as it could have been. Laws had been passed that required new buildings be strong enough to withstand earthquakes. And since 1989, bridges in the area have been strengthened, as well. San Francisco intends to be ready the next time there is a major quake.

But no one can really predict the timing of the next one. Nor is there a way to tell how powerful it will be. All that's known is that sooner or later, it will come.

Ring of Fire

The Ring of Fire is an imaginary line around the Pacific Ocean. About 90 percent of the world's earthquakes occur along this ring.

Why is that?

The ring is where several of the earth's tectonic plates meet. The ring starts at the southern tip of South America. It runs northward all the way to Alaska. Then it crosses to Russia and goes south, following the coast of East Asia. It runs through the nations of Japan, the Philippines, and Indonesia.

The world's largest recorded earthquake was along the Ring of Fire, in Chile, in 1960. The western coast of the United States lies within the Ring of Fire. The most powerful earthquake in the United States took place in 1964 in Alaska, and measured 9.2 on the Richter scale.

Timeline for San Francisco

1769	San Francisco Bay area is claimed by Spain
1776	The Presidio and Mission Dolores are founded
1840s–1850s	Chinese laborers are recruited to work in mines and build railroads
1848	Gold is discovered in California
1850	California becomes a state
1869	Leland Stanford drives in the Golden Spike, joining the Central Pacific and Union Pacific railroads to create the Transcontinental Railroad
1900–c. 1908	Outbreak of bubonic plague in San Francisco, brought by ships sailing from the Far East
1901	Theodore Roosevelt becomes president of the United States
1906	San Francisco earthquake
1915	Panama-Pacific International Exposition (World's Fair)
1935	Charles F. Richter proposes the Richter scale
1937	The Golden Gate Bridge opens
1958	The New York Giants move to San Francisco
1967	The hippies' "Summer of Love"
1972	The Transamerica Pyramid opens
1973	Alcatraz Federal Penitentiary is opened to the public

1978	Mayor George Moscone and Supervisor Harvey Milk are killed by Supervisor Dan White
1989	The Loma Prieta earthquake disrupts on live TV the third game of the World Series between the San Francisco Giants and the Oakland A's
2011	Edwin Lee elected first Chinese American mayor of major American city
2014	San Francisco Giants win the World Series for the third time in five years

Timeline for the Earthquakes in World History

1556 — An estimated 8.0 earthquake in Shaanxi, China, is considered the deadliest in history with over eight hundred thousand killed

c. 1700 — The oral histories of First Nations and Native American tribes record an estimated 9.0 quake that jolts the West Coast of North America

1730 — Few casualties result from an estimated 8.7 earthquake in Valparaiso, Chile, as people had fled their homes after earlier tremors

1755 — An estimated 8.7 earthquake destroys Lisbon, Portugal, and leads to the birth of scientific studies of earthquakes

1868 — Arica, Peru, is rocked by an estimated 9.0 earthquake that creates a tsunami, which travels all the way to New Zealand

1906 — An earthquake estimated at 8.8 hits the coast of Ecuador, and the resulting tsunami causes damage as far away as Japan

1950 — The Assam-Tibet earthquake is calculated at 8.6. Landslides destroy about seventy villages

1952 — A tsunami caused by a 9.0 earthquake on the Kamchatka Peninsula, Russia, causes a million dollars in damage in Hawaii

1957	An 8.6 hits the Andreanof Islands, Alaska, and causes Mt. Vsevidof to erupt
1960	The most powerful earthquake ever recorded, a 9.5 in Chile, causes damage of more than a billion dollars
1964	The biggest known earthquake in North America, a 9.2 in Alaska, triggers landslides that cause heavy damage to Anchorage
1965	An 8.7 is recorded at Rat Island, Alaska, and a tsunami travels all the way to Japan
2004	The 9.1 Sumatra-Andaman earthquake causes the deadliest tsunami ever recorded, devastating countries all around the Indian Ocean
2010	An 8.8 earthquake off the shore of Bio-Bio, Chile, causes $30 billion worth of damage
2011	Japan is hit by a 9.0 earthquake, setting off a tsunami that sweeps away villages and causes a nuclear meltdown in a damaged power plant in Fukushima
2015	A 7.8 earthquake in Nepal moves Mount Everest more than an inch to the southwest

Bibliography

*Books for young readers

Fradkin, Philip L. *The ___ ___ Earthquake and Firestorms of 1906.*
    Berkeley: Unive___ ___ 2005.

Kennedy, John Cast___ ___ ___ San
    Francisco, 19___

Kurzman, Dan. *D___ ___ ___quake
    and Fire o___ ___.*

Morris, Charles ___ ___ *___quake and*
    Fire. Sec___ ___ lished in
    1906.)

Smith, Dennis. *San Franci___ ___ ___told Story of*
    the 1906 Earthquake and Fires. Ne___ ___ Viking, 2005.

* Tanaka, Shelley. *A Day That Changed America: Earthquake!*
    New York: Hyperion, 2004.

Thomas, Gordon, and Max Morgan Witts. *The San Francisco*
    Earthquake. New York: Stein and Day, 1971.

Winchester, Simon. *A Crack in the Edge of the World.* New York:
    HarperCollins, 2005.

31901064634597